Sage instant accounting explained

OTHER TITLES OF INTEREST

Sage instant accounting explained

By

David Weale

BERNARD BABANI (publishing) LTD
THE GRAMPIANS
SHEPHERDS BUSH ROAD
LONDON W6 7NF
ENGLAND

PLEASE NOTE

Although every care has been taken with the production of this book to ensure that any instructions or any of the other contents operate in a correct and safe manner, the Author and the Publishers do not accept any responsibility for any failure, damage or loss caused by following the said contents. The Author and Publisher do not take any responsibility for errors or omissions.

The Author and Publisher will not be liable to the purchaser or to any other person or legal entity with respect to any liability, loss or damage (whether direct, indirect, special, incidental or consequential) caused or alleged to be caused directly or indirectly by this book.

The book is sold as is, without any warranty of any kind, either expressed or implied, respecting the contents, including but not limited to implied warranties regarding the book's quality, performance, correctness or fitness for any particular purpose.

© 1996 BERNARD BABANI (publishing) LTD

First published - February 1996

British Library Cataloguing in Publication Data

Weale. D
Sage Instant Accounting Explained
1.Title
657 . 0285536 9

ISBN 0 85934 398 7

Cover design by Gregor Arthur
Cover illustration by Adam Willis
Printed and bound in Great Britain by Cox & Wyman Ltd, Reading.

TRADEMARKS

SAGE Instant Accounting is a registered trademark of SAGE PLC.

ABOUT THE AUTHOR

David Weale is a Fellow of the Institute of Chartered Accountants and has worked in both private and public practice. At present he is a lecturer in business computing at Yeovil College.

Apart from computing his interests are running and music.

He lives in Somerset with his wife, three children and Siamese cat.

DEDICATION

This book is dedicated to my wife for putting up with me all these years, with love.

Contents

THE MODULE BUTTONS..49

Introduction

This book is intended to explain how to make best use of SAGE Instant Accounting.

It is not supposed to be, in any way, a replacement or substitute for the manual that comes with the program but is a supplementary text that could help the user to understand the program.

It could be used by anyone having bought the program who wants a simple explanatory text or by someone thinking of buying the program who wants to see how it works.

For the purposes of this book it is assumed that the reader is familiar with the WINDOWS environment. If you are not, then you need to consult the WINDOWS manual or a book on the subject or attend a course.

I hope you enjoy it.

David Weale February 1996

How the program can help you

Sage Instant Accounting is designed to be a simple to use and very effective financial tool for your business.

It contains most of the features found in the more sophisticated version of the Sage programs such as Sage Accountant or Financial Controller (although some of the features within Instant Accounting offer fewer options). Indeed the data you enter will be usable if you upgrade at any time.

The program contains the following modules:

Customers
You enter customer details, record invoices and produce reports, keep track of how much you are owed and how long the money has been owed to you. You can also use this option to send letters to your customers (for example to request payment).

Suppliers
Similar to Customers, you keep details of your suppliers and how much you owe to them, for how long.

Nominal
This option keeps track of all transactions that are allocated to the different codes you are using. You can produce useful graphs and charts to help you see how your business is performing.

Bank
You use this option to record all moneys paid or received by you. It can also be used for credit card transactions and for cash transactions. You can reconcile any of these accounts.

Products
Here your stock is recorded. You can see the items you hold in stock and their prices. Details from this are used in the Invoicing option to print your invoices.

Invoicing
Use this to print invoices and credit notes to your customers and to automatically update your ledgers.

Financials
This is where you print or view your accounts, set budgets and calculate your VAT return or compare this year's figures with last year's. This information is vital for the successful management of your financial affairs.

Reports
Standard financial reports are produced using this option, for example the Audit Trail (a list of every transaction you have recorded).

Help
As with all Windows programs, there is a help button that will give you specific assistance.

Accounting Terminology

If you are new to the idea of accounts or unclear about some of the specialised terms used then this chapter will help.

I have explained the terms used in accounting so that you can see how SAGE Instant Accounting fits into the accounting framework.

To begin we will look at the accounts produced by the program, this is followed by an explanation of the ledgers, double-entry book-keeping, VAT accounting and other useful techniques used within the program.

The Accounts

Profit & Loss Account
This shows how successful your business is over a specified time (for example a year).

From the Sales are deducted the Purchases and Direct Expenses, the result is called the Gross Profit.

Then all the overheads you have incurred during the period are listed, totalled and deducted from the Gross Profit. The resulting figure is called the Net Profit.

This can be produced as often as you wish, for example monthly or yearly. The profit (or loss) shows how well the business has traded.

Profit & Loss

	This Month	Year to Date
Sales		
Product Sales	XXXXXX.XX	XXXXXX.XX
Export Sales	XXXXXX.XX	XXXXXX.XX
Sales of Assets	XXXXXX.XX	XXXXXX.XX
Other Sales	XXXXXX.XX	XXXXXX.XX
	XXXXXX.XX	XXXXXX.XX
Purchases		
Purchases	XXXXXX.XX	XXXXXX.XX
Purchase Charges	XXXXXX.XX	XXXXXX.XX
Stock	XXXXXX.XX	XXXXXX.XX
	XXXXXX.XX	XXXXXX.XX
Direct Expenses		
Labour	XXXXXX.XX	XXXXXX.XX
Commissions	XXXXXX.XX	XXXXXX.XX
Sales Promotion	XXXXXX.XX	XXXXXX.XX
Miscellaneous Exp	XXXXXX.XX	XXXXXX.XX
	XXXXXX.XX	XXXXXX.XX
Gross Profit	XXXXXX.XX	XXXXXX.XX
Overheads		
Salaries & Wages	XXXXXX.XX	XXXXXX.XX
Rent and Rates	XXXXXX.XX	XXXXXX.XX
Heat & Power	XXXXXX.XX	XXXXXX.XX
Motor Expenses	XXXXXX.XX	XXXXXX.XX
Travelling/Ent	XXXXXX.XX	XXXXXX.XX
Printing/Stat	XXXXXX.XX	XXXXXX.XX
Prof. Fees	XXXXXX.XX	XXXXXX.XX
Equipment Hire	XXXXXX.XX	XXXXXX.XX
Maintenance	XXXXXX.XX	XXXXXX.XX
Bank Charges	XXXXXX.XX	XXXXXX.XX
Depreciation	XXXXXX.XX	XXXXXX.XX
Bad Debts	XXXXXX.XX	XXXXXX.XX
General Expenses	XXXXXX.XX	XXXXXX.XX
	XXXXXX.XX	XXXXXX.XX
Net Profit	XXXXXX.XX	XXXXXX.XX

Balance Sheet

Unlike the Profit & Loss Account that covers a period of time, the Balance Sheet shows the assets and liabilities of your business at a specific date.

The **Year To** figures are the cumulative figures for the year to date.

```
Balance Sheet
                            This Month         Year to

Fixed Assets
Property                    XXXXXX.XX          XXXXXX.XX
Plant and Machinery         XXXXXX.XX          XXXXXX.XX
Office Equipment            XXXXXX.XX          XXXXXX.XX
Furniture & Fixtures        XXXXXX.XX          XXXXXX.XX
Motor Vehicles              XXXXXX.XX          XXXXXX.XX

                            XXXXXX.XX          XXXXXX.XX
Current Assets
Stock                       XXXXXX.XX          XXXXXX.XX
Debtors                     XXXXXX.XX          XXXXXX.XX
Deposits and Cash           XXXXXX.XX          XXXXXX.XX
Bank Account                XXXXXX.XX          XXXXXX.XX
VAT Liability               XXXXXX.XX          XXXXXX.XX

                            XXXXXX.XX          XXXXXX.XX
Current Liabilities
Creditors : Short Term      XXXXXX.XX          XXXXXX.XX
Taxation                    XXXXXX.XX          XXXXXX.XX
Creditors : Long Term       XXXXXX.XX          XXXXXX.XX
Bank Account                XXXXXX.XX          XXXXXX.XX
VAT Liability               XXXXXX.XX          XXXXXX.XX

                            XXXXXX.XX          XXXXXX.XX
Net Current Assets          XXXXXX.XX          XXXXXX.XX
Net Assets                  XXXXXX.XX          XXXXXX.XX

Financed By
Share Capital               XXXXXX.XX          XXXXXX.XX
Reserves                    XXXXXX.XX          XXXXXX.XX
Profit / Loss Account       XXXXXX.XX          XXXXXX.XX
B/Fwd Profit                XXXXXX.XX          XXXXXX.XX
                            XXXXXX.XX          XXXXXX.XX
```

Assets are the items your business owns and Liabilities are the items or amount your business owes to others.

Assets are divided into two types, Fixed and Current.

Fixed Assets
Normally assets that will be retained for some time, examples are buildings (property), office equipment.

Current Assets
Assets that are temporary in nature, for example bank accounts, cash, debtors (customers who owe you money).

Liabilities are amounts due to others.

Net Assets
This represents the difference between total assets and total liabilities.

Financed By
This represents the money invested by you in the business **plus** the reserves and the profit or loss.

By definition a Balance Sheet **must** balance, for example the Net Assets must be equal to the total of the Financed By section. Luckily with computerised accounts it is difficult not to balance.

The Ledgers

The day to day transactions of a business are recorded in ledgers. There are three main ledgers, Sales, Purchases and Nominal.

Sales Ledger

SAGE calls this CUSTOMERS that is a much more sensible description.

This ledger records all transactions with your individual customers. A separate account within the ledger is opened for each customer and all transactions for that customer are recorded in that account, for example invoices sent to the customer, credit notes and payments received from the customer.

The balance on the customer's account represents the amount the customer owes to you.

The total of all the balances in all the customer accounts represents the total debtors' figure and is shown as the DEBTORS CONTROL ACCOUNT in the NOMINAL ledger.

Purchase Ledger

Again SAGE has renamed this as SUPPLIERS and it is used to record your transactions with each of your suppliers.

It operates in a very similar way to the SALES ledger and the total of all the balances on all the individual supplier accounts is the CREDITORS CONTROL ACCOUNT. This represents the total amount you owe to your suppliers at any time.

Nominal Ledger

This summarises all the financial data from the SALES and PURCHASE ledgers and from other financial records such as the cash book and bank.

The TRIAL BALANCE is made up from the balances of the individual nominal ledger accounts and is used to produce the Profit & Loss Account and the Balance Sheet.

Double-Entry Accounting

All accounting systems whether manual or computerised use the **double-entry system** to record the transactions. This means that all data is recorded twice, once as a debit and once as a credit entry (in different accounts).

With computerised systems the mechanics of the double-entry system are carried out automatically and the system is therefore self balancing. When you look at some of the statements and reports generated by SAGE you will see two columns, the left headed **DB** or **Debit** and the right **CR** or **Credit**.

For your interest a **debit** entry increases the value of a Balance Sheet asset or increases an expenditure account in the Profit & Loss account.

Conversely a **credit** entry reduces the value of an asset, increases the value of a liability or increases an income account.

VAT

All businesses with a certain turnover have to register with the Customs & Excise for VAT. When you register you are allocated a VAT Registration number that you must quote on all your documentation.

If registered you must charge VAT on all goods or services (that are chargeable to VAT - not all are) and you can set against this all VAT you pay on goods or services supplied to you.

The difference between the Input and Output VAT has to be paid to the C&E (or possibly reclaimed).

It is the law that you must keep detailed records of your VAT for inspection by C&E officers. SAGE does this for you (provided you enter the transactions correctly).

Budgets

Once you have entered the data into the program then as well as producing the accounts you can produce information that may help you manage your business more effectively.

A method of keeping control of your finances is to use budgets. You set budgets for any or all of your different types of income and expenditure. These budgets can be set using the previous year's figures or estimates that you have made. As the year progresses you can look at reports showing the budgeted and the actual figures with the difference or variance also shown.

The advantage of this is being able quickly to see where you have large differences between budget and actual and then being able to do something about it before it is too late.

Bank Reconciliations

You can reconcile the figures in your computerised accounts against the actual bank statements to ensure that the bank statement is correct. You can add any necessary items to the computerised system, for example bank charges.

Credit Control

Another feature that enables you to manage your business better is credit control. This allows you to set credit limits and to monitor your customer accounts so that you may not get in the situation where a customer owes you too much money for too long a period.

This feature also enables you to send statements and reminders to your customers and to produce aged debtors' lists.

Legal Requirements

Every business or trading organisation is required, by law, to maintain accounting records to show and explain all financial transactions. At the very least these must show the date, amount and purpose of all payments in or out of the business plus the assets and liabilities and the stock value at any time. Also details of all goods bought or sold to customers or suppliers must be recorded

Windows Conventions

There are several buttons used within all Windows screens with which you should be familiar.

 You can exit from the section you are using (or the program itself) by clicking on the symbol in the top left hand corner of the window and selecting CLOSE.

 Clicking on this button reduces the window you are using to an icon, to enlarge the icon click on it. Then choose the relevant option from the menu shown (for example MAXIMISE will enlarge the window to full screen).

 Clicking on this button makes the window full screen.

 This reduces a full screen window to its previous size.

Using the scroll bars

Some of the dialog boxes have scroll bars, these have an arrow at the top and bottom and you click on the arrows to move up or down the list shown within the dialog box.

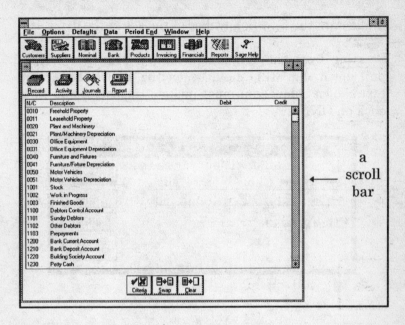

a
scroll
bar

Scroll bars also appear along the bottom of some windows and dialog boxes.

Installing the program

You may have the program already installed on your computer, however you may not, or you may want to re-install it.

Make sure the first floppy disc of the set in the drive.

Starting from the Windows Program Manager screen, pull down the FILE menu, selecting RUN. Enter the text shown below (you must include the colon) and then click on OK.

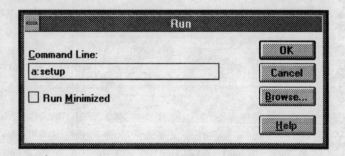

You will see the following screen. You can either install for the first time **or** just install the program files that will not affect any existing data.

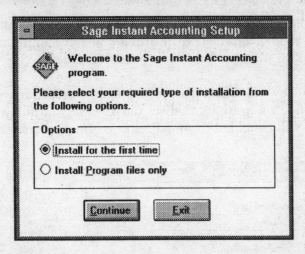

If are installing for the first time you will see a dialog box into which you can enter the necessary details.

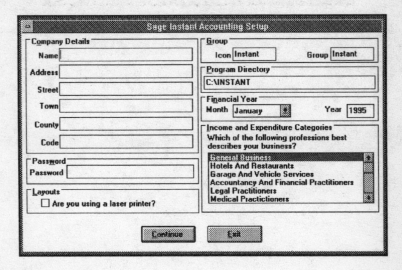

Note the selection on the bottom right, you can select the most appropriate categories for your particular business.

Also note that you set the financial year, it is possible to alter it at a later stage (**before** you have entered any data).

From now on follow the prompts, the program will be installed on your hard disc and the Sage window and icons will be added to your Program Manager screen.

The Sage Instant Window

Sage Instant Accounting has its Windows group in the Program Manager Screen. It looks like this:

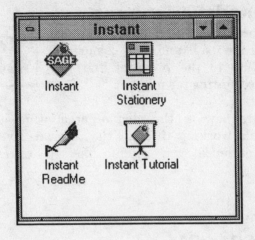

The other Sage icons

Within the Sage Instant Window are three other icons.

The Tutorial

The Tutorial is totally separate from the program itself and is a colourful introduction to the program and to certain accounting terms.

If you are new to the idea of accounting it is well worthwhile working through the tutorial. Even if you have experience you might like to refresh your knowledge.

Instant ReadMe

This file contains information that is not contained within the manual and you would do well to read and print it before using the program itself.

Instant Stationery

You can use this option to design and order pre-printed stationery from Sage. The program takes you through the design stage and lets you see how it would look before ordering it.

Loading The Program

To load the program click twice (quickly), using the left hand mouse button, on the **Instant** icon and the program will begin to load.

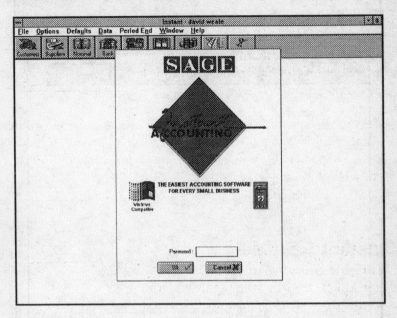

The initial screen includes a password if you have installed one (it is possible to do this at any time).

After entering your password you will see the MAIN MENU screen. You select your option by clicking on your choice of icon.

There are also pull down menus that can be accessed by clicking on any of the commands shown along the top of the screen.

As you can see it is a normal Windows layout with pull down menus and buttons.

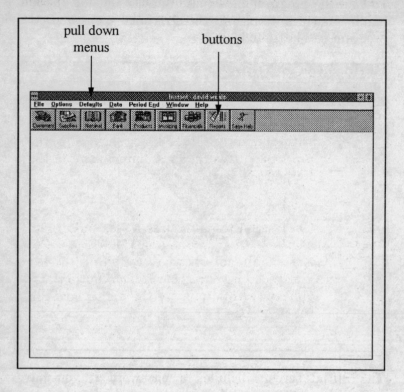

Sage Specifics

There are buttons and other commands specific to Sage programs, some are dealt with here, the less used ones are covered in the appendices.

Dialog Box buttons

 When you click on this button you will be presented with a list. This button appears within many of the dialog boxes in the program. It works in a similar way to the **F4** function key.

 Clicking on this produces a set of alternate choices. To choose one of these instead of the one already shown, scroll down the list and click on your choice. This button also appears within many of the dialog boxes in the program.

 Within some of the dialog boxes you can, if you wish, set criteria for your choice. For example you may choose only those customers owing more than a certain amount of money.

 This swaps the selection to the other (deselected) records.

 This clears the Criteria selection.

Other dialog boxes

The dialog boxes within SAGE contain additional buttons, normally along the bottom of the dialog box. The following are common to most modules (although they do not all individually appear in all the dialog boxes).

Save

This enables you to save the current dialog box, for example a customer record.

Abandon

If you make a mistake in the data entry then you can abandon it and start again. This button has the effect of clearing the data without saving it.

Prev / Next

If you have selected all the records then these buttons let you move from the current one to the next or previous.

Delete

You can delete the current (record). There is usually another screen to check that you are certain you want to delete the item.

Memo

This lets you add suitable text to the item.

Close

Use this option to return to the previous menu after having finished with the current screen.

Selecting records

You may want to look at or alter the details of certain of your customers or suppliers. Many of the dialog boxes display a list of items, for example customer names or nominal codes.

You can select any of these by clicking the mouse pointer on them.

To select more than one simply click again and you will see that both are highlighted (and so on if you want to select more).

To alter the selection you can deselect by clicking the mouse on the item again or you can use the available buttons.

Hint:
☐ To sort the data double-click the mouse pointer on the heading of the column you want sorted (hold the SHIFT key down at the same time for a reverse order sort). The sorted data will revert to its original state when you close down the window.

Moving around the dialog boxes

When you enter data or other details within any of the screens you can use either of the following techniques.

☐ Within each dialog box you can either click the mouse or you can TAB between each field.

☐ To move up (or backwards) within the dialog box hold down the SHIFT key and then press the TAB key.

Function Keys

Sage makes use of the function keys on your keyboard, here is a table of them.

F1	Brings up the HELP screens
F2	Displays the calculator
F4	Displays a list of alternate choices e.g. A/C codes
F5	Inserts the current (system) date
F6	Deletes / resets the entry within some fields
F11	Loads the WINDOWS Control Panel
F12	Loads WINDOWS WRITE (to edit layouts)

Sage Instant Help

Throughout the program there are explanations and hints that appear automatically when you leave the mouse pointer on a button or data entry field for a few seconds.

Hint:
□ You can quickly start the Instant Help by clicking the **right hand** mouse button.

An example is shown below.

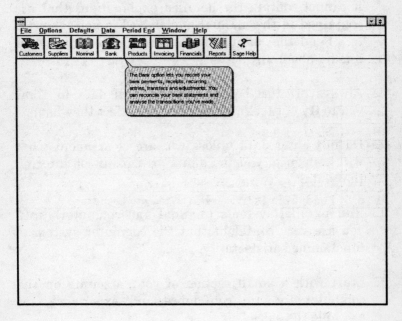

Some words of warning

Before you begin to use the program there are several tips you would do well to read and digest.

☐ Before making any alteration to the program defaults or entering any data, you may like to make a backup of the program files.

☐ Always backup your data files on a regular basis.

☐ This book is not a substitute for reading the manual, it cannot contain the detailed explanations that are contained in the manual and indeed is not supposed to. Read the manual if you are at all confused or unsure about any activity.

☐ Always practise before entering real data to allow you to try out techniques to see the effect they have.

☐ Do **not** enter data unless you are clear about what will happen to your accounts as a result of entering that data.

☐ Run parallel systems (manual and computer) until you are very confident that the computer system is functioning satisfactorily.

☐ Start with a small section of your accounts on the computer to gain confidence and experience, for example the sales ledger.

☐ Use your accountant's knowledge and skill to help you.

☐ Subscribe to the SAGE help line. This is very useful, you can phone for any help you need and will get information about upgrades.

The Pull Down Menus

Clicking on any of these leads to a (pull down) menu. From this list you select the command you want.

Within each pull down menu you can select the command you want by clicking on it with the mouse or by moving the cursor onto it by using the cursor control keys and then pressing the RETURN key.

File Menu

From this you have the following choices.

Printer Setup
If you have set up more than one printer this option lets you select the one you want to use for the output.

Exit
Choose this if you want to exit from SAGE.

Options Menu

Customers
Suppliers
Nominal Ledger
Bank
Products
Invoicing
Financials
Reports
Sage Help

This menu is an alternative to the use of the buttons in selecting any of the modules making up the program

You can also turn off (or on) the Instant Help by clicking on the Sage Help command button in the toolbar.

Defaults Menu

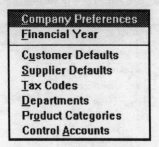

These are the original settings that come with SAGE. You can alter them if you so wish and then your settings become the defaults.

Company Preferences

These are set when you install the program. As you can see from the illustration, the screen shows the name, address and password, any of which you can alter.

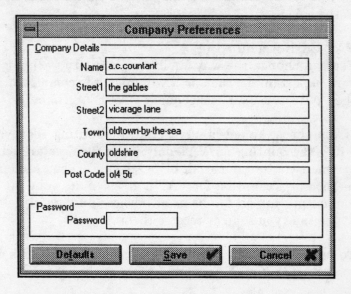

Note the button on the left of the dialog box, this enables you to alter the defaults shown below.

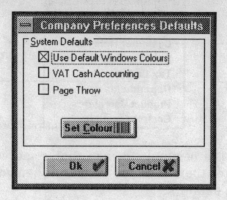

Use Default Windows Colours (Set Colour)
Many happy hours can be spent altering the colours that are shown on the screen. You will be given a palette of colours that you can select as you wish. To SET COLOUR you must turn off the USE DEFAULT COLOURS option (by clicking on it so that there is no X in the box).

VAT Cash Accounting
You can change the way VAT is accounted for, this is a very important decision as it will affect the completion of the VAT returns and consequently your VAT liability.

If you choose to select VAT Cash Accounting then you will be accounting for VAT only when invoices are paid or when you buy for cash or by cheque. (The standard method of accounting for VAT is to calculate your input and output tax on the basis of invoices and credit notes at the time you send or receive them).

To select VAT Cash Accounting (if you so decide) click on the box so that an X appears.

It is essential that you discuss how to account for VAT with your accountant. A change to Cash Accounting can only be made with prior agreement of your local VAT office.

Once you have started to post invoices you cannot switch back from VAT cash accounting.

Page Throw
If this is selected a new page will be started for (history) reports for each account.

Financial Year
You can alter the start of the financial year within this, but only if you have not posted any data.

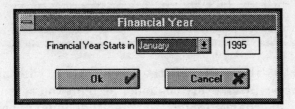

Customer Defaults

Selecting this allow you to alter the default settings for customers.

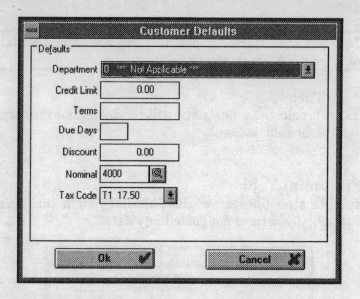

You can alter any of these and they will appear automatically on every customer account you set up, you can also change them on an individual basis as necessary.

It would be sensible to set up the defaults for the most used data and then you only have to alter some of the individual accounts.

Supplier Defaults

The same comments apply to this as to the Customer Defaults above.

Tax Codes

This displays a dialog box that allows you to alter the active (usable) codes and the VAT rate applicable to them.

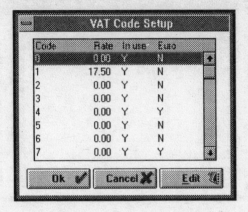

To change any of the codes highlight them and then click on the EDIT button.

Sage recommends the following codes are used and the progam uses these to calculate the VAT return.

T0	zero rated
T1	standard rate
T2	exempt
T4	standard rate sales to EC customers
T7	zero rate purchases from EC
T8	standard rate purchases from EC
T9	non vat transactions

You can enter the details and then click on OK to save them. You should then see the relevant figures and selections change within the VAT Code Setup box.

Note that only codes T4, T7 and T8 are used by the program in calculating EC VAT Returns.

Departments

Here you can setup the departmental structure you want.

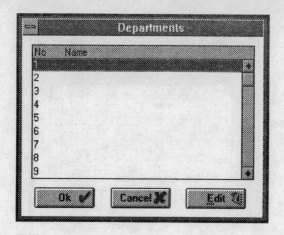

To create departments simply click on the number and then on the EDIT button. Enter the name you want to call the department and then on the OK button and you will see it included in the list.

This is really for information, to produce reports by department you would need to do it manually or upgrade the program.

Product Categories

This works in a very similar way to DEPARTMENTS, however you can use the **Criteria** button to produce reports for specific product categories.

Control Accounts

You can alter the code for any of the displayed control accounts, however I would think very seriously before doing so.

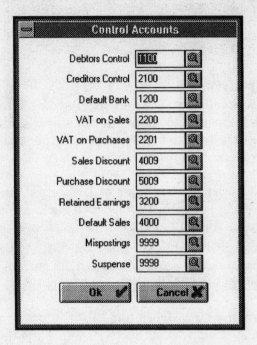

You cannot alter the code for most control accounts once any data has been entered.

Data menu

You have three choices.

Backup/Restore

It is **essential** that you BACKUP your data files; if anything happened to these your business could rapidly become a disaster area. The most effective security is to regularly backup your data files.

This could work on the basis of keeping **at least** three generations of backups. Each set of backup files should be kept in a separate location (at least one being kept away from the office).

Always **label** the backup discs clearly

The generations may work like this:

☐ A backup is made using a new set of discs

☐ Next day another backup is made

☐ The following day a third backup is made

☐ The fourth day the first backup is re-used

☐ The fifth day the second backup is re-used.

☐ A weekly backup is also made on the same principles as above

So whether you choose to back up daily or weekly (or in between) you are keeping three sets of backups on the go.

Another possibility is to keep a daily backup for a week (five sets) and a weekly backup for the last four weeks and a monthly backup for the last six months (or whatever permutations you choose).

The RESTORE option lets you replace corrupted files (or to replace horrible mistakes) with the last version of your files that you backed up.

There is a considerable difference between BACKUP and RESTORE; if you confuse them then you could end up with no data files at all.

The BACKUP dialog box looks like this.

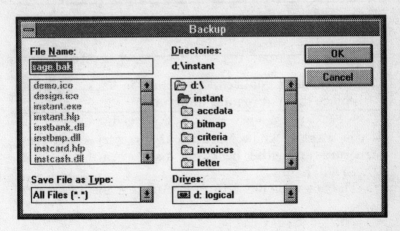

It is not a good idea to back up to the hard disc (which is the default) as if you have a problem with it you may not be able to access your files at all !.

Ideally you should backup to a floppy disc **(Drive a:)**. When doing so you must make sure you have a formatted and empty disc in the drive before starting.

During the backup process you will see the following display, which shows the backup taking place.

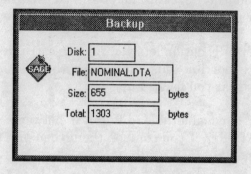

Remember to BACKUP regularly and consistently.

The RESTORE option follows a similar pattern.

Hint:
☐ Buy the best quality discs for use in backing up and replace them at regular intervals.

If you want to know more about directories and their structure any good book on disc operating systems (DOS) will help.

Oops !

This is a diagnostic feature of the program that will check and correct errors within your SAGE files and allows you to correct certain mistakes.

There are three options.

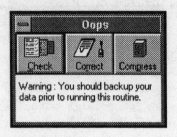

Please note the warning.

Check
The SAGE manual contains several pages of instructions if this option finds problems with your data files. Unless you are happy to carry out the instructions, I would suggest calling in an expert.

Correct
This part of the DISK DOCTOR helps you alter misposted data.

Only some data fields can be changed using this option.

When you select the CORRECT option you will be shown the AUDIT TRAIL and you can scroll down this to select the transaction you want to alter.

To do this, highlight the item and then select the EDIT button, make the alteration (if possible) and click on the OK button.

If you alter the transaction date you may also have to alter the payment date.

You can also reverse a transaction using this feature by altering the value to ZERO. This will effectively mean that the transaction never took place. These changes will show up on the AUDIT TRAIL.

If the VAT has changed then it may be best to carry out a reverse posting, i.e. zero the original values and enter the transaction again.

There are various restrictions with this option and a thorough reading of the SAGE program manual would be wise before attempting to alter the data.

Whenever carrying out these corrections it would be very sensible to print out the AUDIT TRAIL to ensure that the effect of the changes is what you want to happen. Remember if in doubt ask your accountant to check.

Compress
You can use this option to compress the data files so that empty records are deleted and the file size is reduced.

This is IRREVERSIBLE, so you **must** BACKUP your data files before attempting this.

Period End menu

There are two options here as shown below.

Month End

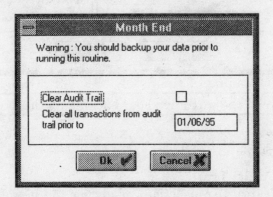

Note the warning just below the title on the screen. Backing up has already been dealt with in an earlier section and is a **VERY IMPORTANT** aspect of any computer system, ignore it at your peril.

You can clear the Audit trail of certain completed transactions, i.e. reconciled and fully paid transactions.

Year End

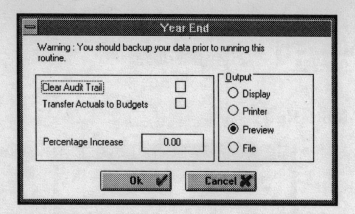

Again read the warning about backing up the data.

You can choose to.

Clear Audit Trail
Clears certain transactions ready for the new financial year.

Transfer Actuals to Budgets
This allows you to set the actual figures spent this year as the budget for next, optionally setting a percentage increase for next year's budgets (PERCENTAGE INCREASE).

Window menu

These are standard WINDOWS commands that arrange
the (open) windows on the screen.

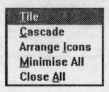

The one that I find most useful is CLOSE ALL which
closes all the open windows returning to the MAIN
MENU.

It is worthwhile experimenting with each of the
commands if you are unfamiliar with them.

Help menu

This follows the normal Windows conventions. The INDEX screen is shown below which can also be accessed by function key **F1**.

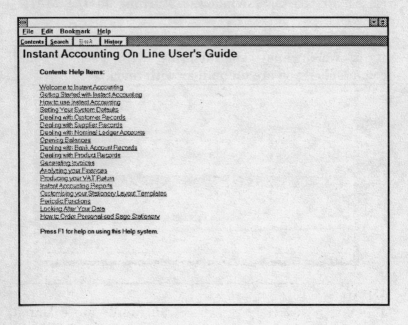

Searching for help

You can also search for help by clicking on the SEARCH command.

You then type in the topic you are interested in (or scroll down the list) and click on the SHOW TOPICS. Then after selecting the relevant topic, click on the GOTO button and a screen will be displayed with the required help.

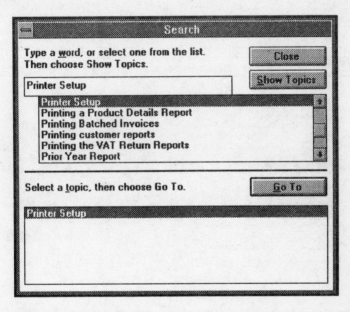

Hints:

☐ Within any Help screen certain words are coloured green. If you move the cursor onto them a hand will appear.

☐ Those fully underlined mean that there is a further help screen on that topic, those with a dotted line underneath lead to a text box explaining the word or phrase.

Context sensitive help

The program includes context sensitive help. This means that if you press the **F1** key from anywhere within the program, you should be given help on that section of the program.

The Module Buttons

The buttons on the main screen give you access to all the individual modules or components of the program. You can see the buttons on the display above.

Each of these will be looked at in sequence.

Customers

The CUSTOMERS option is the Sage equivalent of the SALES ledger. The initial screen looks like this.

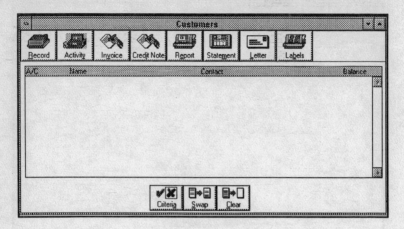

As you can see the CUSTOMERS module screen has several new buttons. We will identify each in turn.

Record

This option lets you set up the details for each customer. You have to enter certain data into each customer's record before saving it.

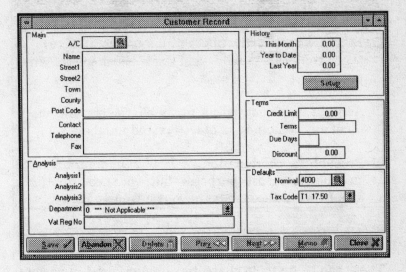

A/C

Each customer must be allocated an A/C code. This code will be used throughout the program to both call up the customer details and to analyse the accounts.

Each code must be unique (in fact if you try to use an already existing code the screen will fill up with the details you have entered for that code).

Hints:

☐ Considerable thought should be given to the allocation of account codes, the more carefully and logically you do this, the more structured and workable your system will be.

☐ It is always worthwhile arranging the structure so that you can easily add new customers when necessary.

☐ Account codes can be up to six characters and made up of any combination of letters and numbers.

☐ Probably a combination of letters and numbers is suitable for most purposes but you need to think about this in the context of your business.

Name / Street 1 / Street 2 / Town / County / Post Code

These can be up to 30 characters and are used in various parts of the program including stationery and address labels.

Obviously every customer will need to be entered and you may wish to have several records for some customers where you are dealing with different branches or departments of that customer (be careful with the A/C codes).

Contact

The person you normally deal with, again this can be up to 30 characters long and can be printed on address labels.

Telephone / Fax

The customer's number.

Analysis

These three fields let you analyse the account by certain criteria. This can be used within the reporting structure to produce detailed reports.

Department

You can allocate the customer to a specific department within your organisation.

Tax ID

Your customer's Country Code and VAT number.

This Month

This shows the total figure for transactions that have been entered in the current month, it is zeroed when the MONTH END option is used.

Year to Date

The total transactions for the year to date, it is zeroed by the running the YEAR END option.

Last Year

This figure automatically results from running the YEAR END option and is the total transaction figure for the previous financial year. You can enter it yourself if you are starting the program for the first time and do not have a year's figures yet.

Setup

To set up the figures use the SETUP option, you have to save the current record before you can do this.

> This lets you enter outstanding invoices. These are added to the DEBTORS CONTROL ACCOUNT and create a SUSPENSE ACCOUNT balance. A similar process takes place when you use the SETUP option within the SUPPLIERS module only this time they are added to the CREDITORS CONTROL ACCOUNT.

Credit Limit
The amount you want to set for each account. You do not have to set any figure if you do not want to. Entering a figure does not stop you issuing invoices to the customer if the limit is exceeded but it will show up on the AGED analysis (within the ACTIVITY section). An asterisk will be displayed after the account code.

Terms / Due Days / Discount
The trading terms you use with that customer and the number of days they have to pay from the date of the invoice or any settlement discounts. The discount is picked up by the INVOICING module.

Nominal
The sales code for that customer, at present it is set for 4000 but can be altered to any sales code you may wish.

Tax Code
The VAT rate applicable to that customer.

Memo
You can add any additional text you wish.

Activity
You have three choices, the default displays the Turnover for the year to date, the Credit Limit and the Balance on the account. You can also select either AGED or HISTORY.

The AGED display will show the amount owing for each account aged over several different periods.

The HISTORY displays the transactions on the accounts and outstanding items are asterisked, a **P** means partly paid.

Invoice

This option displays a screen that resembles an invoice, this is much more friendly than the traditional accounting programs and makes it easier to enter the information. The screen is shown below.

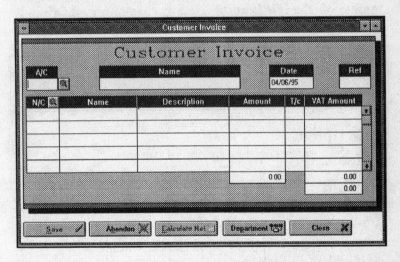

Note that you cannot print an invoice you have entered within this module, it is merely a way of getting the data into the system. If you want to be able to print out the invoice you will need to use the INVOICING module.

A/C

The account code for the customer (remember that you can click on the magnifying glass button to display all the existing codes). Once this has been entered then the name of the customer is automatically entered.

Date
By default this is the system date but it can be altered as necessary.

Ref
You can enter a reference for the invoice

N/C and Name
You do the same with the N/C box.

N/C means the Nominal Code and refers to the code for the item being invoiced. The sales codes are within the 4000 series of codes. Entering a code will produce the name of the N/C automatically assuming it already exists.

Hint:
☐ You can create a new code by selecting NEW from the dialog box that appears.

Description
You then enter the description of the item.

Amount
Enter the amount and the VAT will be calculated (remember to check the VAT rate is correct for that item). The total column will be calculated and the cumulative total also.

Adding items to the invoice
Simply TAB onto the next line of the form and continue as before. You are not limited to the number of items shown initially as you can carry on below. As you enter more items, the cumulative total will alter.

The Buttons
The are several new buttons along the bottom of the window, these are described below.

Calculate Net
Very useful, if you have entered the gross amount, you can click on this button and the VAT will be calculated on the amount and the program will **deduct** the VAT. This could be used if you are only given the amount inclusive of VAT.

Department
You can allocate this invoice to a department within your organisation.

Credit Note
This is the opposite of the Invoice option and the entries are made in the same way.

Report

The initial screen lets you choose from several different reports, five of which are already set up for you.

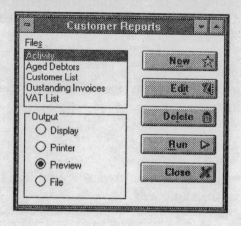

These are reports on Activity (a history of customer transactions), Aged Debtors, Customer List, Outstanding Invoices and VAT List.

The buttons on the right of the dialog box are:

New
This produces the following screen.

Customer Report Creation		
☐ A/C	☐ Fax	☐ Terms
☐ Name	☐ Analysis1	☐ Due Days
☐ Full Address	☐ Analysis2	☐ Tax Code
☐ Street1	☐ Analysis3	☐ Balance (Current)
☐ Street2	☐ Balance	☐ 30 - 60 Days
☐ Town	☐ Credit Limit	☐ 60 - 90 Days
☐ County	☐ This Month	☐ 90 - 120 Days
☐ Post Code	☐ YTD	☐ Balance (Older)
☐ Contact	☐ Last Year	
☐ Telephone		**Report width** [ ]

Save ✔   Cancel ✘

You click on the fields you want to include in the report and then SAVE the form. You will be prompted for a filename that you can decide upon.

Once you have saved this file the name you give it will appear with the other reports.

Edit
This option loads whatever report file you have highlighted from the list. You can then alter the file and save it in its new version.

You cannot edit the fixed (original) reports.

Delete
You can delete any of the files you have created by highlighting them and then choosing this option. There is a further dialog box that asks if you are sure.

You cannot delete the fixed (original) reports.

Run

This will merge the chosen report with the highlighted customers in the box displaying the customers. If no customers are highlighted then all will be included in the report.

Close

Click on this when you have finished with the option and the screen will return to the previous menu.

Output

You can display the report on the screen (DISPLAY) or send it to the PRINTER or to a FILE for future use, you can also PREVIEW it so that you can alter the fonts, etc., before printing out.

Statement

This generates a statement for the selected customers. You can alter the time by changing the Beginning / Ending date and you can choose a different file by using the BROWSE option.

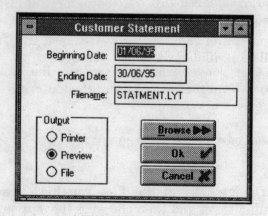

Letter

You can generate a letter requesting payment of an overdue amount or you create your letters using WRITE.

Creating your own letters

This is easy to do and involves either using the **New** button within the LETTER option or using the **F12** function key.

Both call up the Windows WRITE program and Sage has added a VARIABLES option to the EDIT menu that looks like this.

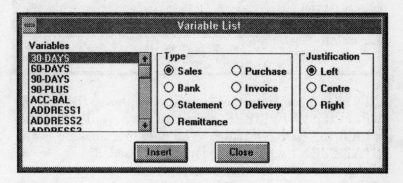

You simply select the variables you want to include within your letter, add the text and save it. The new letter will be available whenever you need it.

Labels

You can print labels to your customers by selecting this option. You can preview the labels, send them to a printer or to a file for future use.

You can change the position of the labels on the page by PREVIEWING them and then selecting the LAYOUT button.

Suppliers

Effectively a mirror image of the CUSTOMERS option. This is the PURCHASE ledger as it is called in traditional accounting systems.

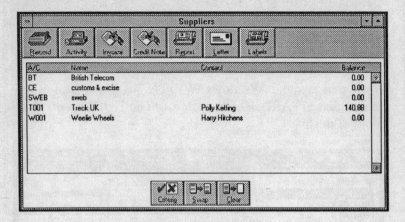

As you can see from the icons shown above, the options within the SUPPLIERS menu are very similar to those within the CUSTOMERS. The only one missing is the STATEMENT which is obviously not needed.

Nominal

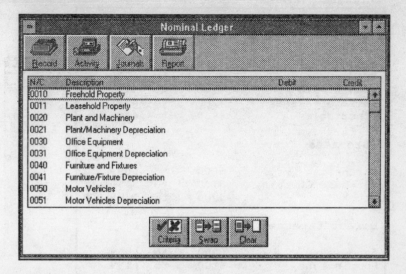

This shows a list of the Nominal Accounts with the debit or credit balance on each.

The codes that come with the program are shown below, these can be deleted, altered and you can add others.

Hint:
☐ If you add codes, make sure they are within the correct range for the activity (for example Sales codes are in the 4000 - 4999 range)

The code groups are shown here:

```
Profit & Loss Account

Sales

Product Sales        4000    to   4099
Export Sales         4100    to   4199
Sales of Assets      4200    to   4299
Other Sales          4900    to   4999

Purchases

Purchases            5000    to   5099
Purchase Charges     5100    to   5199
Stock                5200    to   5299

Direct Expenses

Labour               6000    to   6099
Commissions          6100    to   6199
Sales Promotion      6200    to   6299
Miscellaneous Exps   6900    to   6999

Overheads

Salaries and Wages   7000    to   7099
Rent and Rates       7100    to   7199
Heat, Light & Power  7200    to   7299
Motor Expenses       7300    to   7399
Travelling and Ent   7400    to   7499
Printing/Stationery  7500    to   7599
Professional Fees    7600    to   7699
Equipment Hire       7700    to   7799
Maintenance          7800    to   7899
Bank Charges/Int     7900    to   7999
Depreciation         8000    to   8099
Bad Debts            8100    to   8199
General Expenses     8200    to   8299
```

```
Balance Sheet

Fixed Assets

Property              0010    to   0019
Plant and Machinery   0020    to   0029
Office Equipment      0030    to   0039
Furniture/Fixtures    0040    to   0049
Motor Vehicles        0050    to   0059

Current Assets

Stock                 1000    to   1099
Debtors               1100    to   1199
Deposits and Cash     1210    to   1299
Bank Account          1200    to   1209
VAT Liability         2200    to   2209

Current Liabilities

Creditors:Short       2100    to   2199
Taxation              2210    to   2299
Creditors:Long        2300    to   2399
(Bank Account         1200    to   1209   )
(VAT Liability        2200    to   2209   )

Financed By

Share Capital         3000    to   3099
Reserves              3100    to   3299
```

Over the page are shown all the codes that come with
the program.

Chart of Accounts

0010	Freehold Property	6202	Gifts and Samples
0011	Leasehold Property	6203	P.R. (Literature & Brochures)
0020	Plant and Machinery	6900	Miscellaneous Expenses
0021	Plant/Machinery Depreciation	7001	Directors Salaries
0030	Office Equipment	7002	Directors Remuneration
0031	Office Equipment Depreciation	7003	Staff Salaries
0040	Furniture and Fixtures	7004	Wages - Regular
0041	Furniture/Fixture Depreciation	7005	Wages - Casual
0050	Motor Vehicles	7006	Employers N.I.
0051	Motor Vehicles Depreciation	7007	Employers Pensions
1001	Stock	7008	Recruitment Expenses
1002	Work in Progress	7100	Rent
1003	Finished Goods	7102	Water Rates
1100	Debtors Control Account	7103	General Rates
1101	Sundry Debtors	7104	Premises Insurance
1102	Other Debtors	7200	Electricity
1103	Prepayments	7201	Gas
1200	Bank Current Account	7202	Oil
1210	Bank Deposit Account	7203	Other Heating Costs
1220	Building Society Account	7300	Fuel and Oil
1230	Petty Cash	7301	Repairs and Servicing
2100	Creditors Control Account	7302	Licences
2101	Sundry Creditors	7303	Vehicle Insurance
2102	Other Creditors	7304	Miscellaneous Motor Expenses
2109	Accruals	7400	Travelling
2200	Sales Tax Control Account	7401	Car Hire
2201	Purchase Tax Control Account	7402	Hotels
2202	VAT Liability	7403	U.K. Entertainment
2210	P.A.Y.E.	7404	Overseas Entertainment
2211	National Insurance	7405	Overseas Travelling
2230	Pension Fund	7406	Subsistence
2300	Loans	7500	Printing
2310	Hire Purchase	7501	Postage and Carriage
2320	Corporation Tax	7502	Telephone
2330	Mortgages	7503	Telex/Telegram/Facsimile
3000	Ordinary Shares	7504	Office Stationery
3001	Preference Shares	7505	Books etc.
3100	Reserves	7600	Legal Fees
3101	Undistributed Reserves	7601	Audit and Accountancy Fees
3200	Profit and Loss Account	7602	Consultancy Fees
4000	Sales Type A	7603	Professional Fees
4001	Sales Type B	7700	Equipment Hire
4002	Sales Type C	7701	Office Machine Maintenance
4009	Discounts Allowed	7800	Repairs and Renewals
4100	Sales Type D	7801	Cleaning
4101	Sales Type E	7802	Laundry
4200	Sales of Assets	7803	Premises Expenses
4900	Miscellaneous Income	7900	Bank Interest Paid
4901	Royalties Received	7901	Bank Charges
4902	Commissions Received	7902	Currency Charges
4903	Insurance Claims	7903	Loan Interest Paid
4904	Rent Income	7904	H.P. Interest
4905	Distribution and Carriage	7905	Credit Charges
5000	Materials Purchases	8000	Depreciation
5001	Materials Imported	8001	Plant/Machinery Depreciation
5002	Miscellaneous Purchases	8002	Furniture/Fitting Depreciation
5003	Packaging	8003	Vehicle Depreciation
5009	Discounts Taken	8004	Office Equipment Depreciation
5100	Carriage	8100	Bad Debt Write Off
5101	Import Duty	8102	Bad Debt Provision
5102	Transport Insurance	8200	Donations
5200	Opening Stock	8201	Subscriptions
5201	Closing Stock	8202	Clothing Costs
6000	Productive Labour	8203	Training Costs
6001	Cost of Sales Labour	8204	Insurance
6002	Sub-Contractors	8205	Refreshments
6100	Sales Commissions	9998	Suspense Account
6200	Sales Promotions	9999	Mispostings Account
6201	Advertising		

Record

You can identify a nominal account from the list by clicking on it, you can then record or alter certain data about that account (for example the name you want to call the account) by selecting the RECORD button.

You can also set up totally new account codes that did not previously exist. This is useful as you may have several more types of purchases (for example) than the program has set up for you. To do this enter a new code in the N/C box after selecting the RECORD button.

The opening balance for Nominal Accounts can be SETUP using the SETUP button or can be entered by JOURNAL. The AUDIT TRAIL will show a JD (journal debit) or JC (journal credit) whichever method is used.

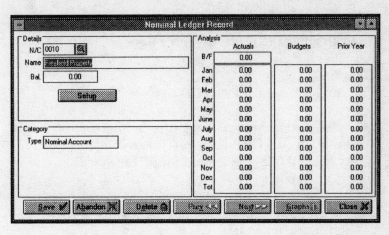

Some of the fields are self explanatory, the others are:

Setup

To set up the details when starting SAGE for the first time (that is the figures that exist before setting it up).

Note the date is always shown as the system date and you may need to alter this.

Actuals

These will be entered automatically by the program as the months go on.

Budget

You enter the budget figures. The beauty of doing this is that the actual and budgeted figures can be compared with each other so that you can easily see any discrepancies and act upon the information.

Prior Year

You can enter the previous year's figures.

Graphs

You can produce graphs of the figures.

A useful option shown along the bottom of the graph screen lets you COPY the chart so that you can include it any WINDOWS application for instance within a word processed report.

You can choose 3D or 2D bar charts as well as line graphs or scatter charts.

Activity

This, like previous modules, lets you display a history of any selected accounts. If you do not select an account all will be displayed in sequence.

Journals

A journal is used to make adjustments to the data you have entered, for example to adjust for VAT at the end of a month.

This is where a knowledge of double entry techniques can be useful.

The data entry screen looks like this.

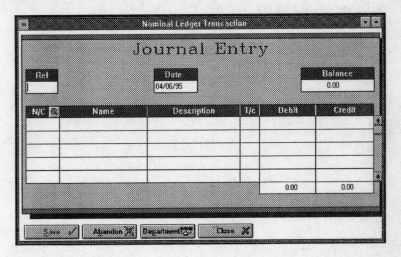

Note you cannot finish or SAVE a journal unless the cumulative total for the debit column is the same as the cumulative total for the credit column, e.g. the balance is zero.

The buttons include one for DEPARTMENT so that you can allocate a journal to a specific department.

Note that the date for the JOURNAL entry (as for all entries into SAGE) is very important as SAGE groups data according to the date of the transaction.

Report

The reporting option follows the same method as the one within the CUSTOMERS option, you can display or edit the existing reports or create your own.

Bank

This deals with the bank accounts of your business. After selecting this the following screen will be displayed.

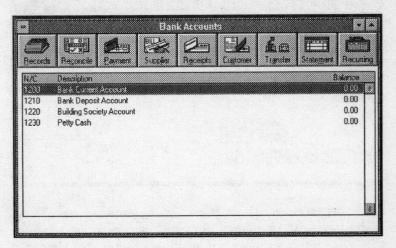

As you can see there is a list of the bank account codes, this includes the defaults and any you create by using the RECORD option.

> **Hint:**
> ☐ You can set up separate bank accounts for different credit card companies you deal with and set up a bank account for cash transactions and these can be reconciled.

Records
This will let you set up new bank accounts.

You can enter any details you wish and then SAVE the result.

Sort Code
This is entered as NN-NN-NN.

Reconciling the bank

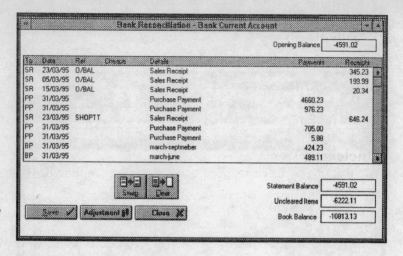

All transactions that have been entered into the computer will be shown for the chosen bank account (only one bank account can be shown at any one time).

The idea is that you reconcile or agree the transactions on your real bank account with those in your computer, by adding additional transactions to adjust for bank charges, interest and any other items that have not been entered into the computer.

The fields are:

Opening Balance
This is the brought forward figure from the previous reconciliation.

Tp
The transaction type.

Date / Ref
The date and reference code for the transaction.

Cheque / Details
The cheque and the details of the transaction.

Payments / Receipts
The amount.

Statement Balance
This should be equal to the book balance after the reconciliation has taken place.

Uncleared Items
A total of the unreconciled amounts that appear on the screen.

Book Balance
The difference between the statement balance and the uncleared items.

How to reconcile

☐ Click on the RECONCILE button, this will display all the recorded transactions in the chosen bank account that have not been previously reconciled.

☐ Note that as you highlight items the STATEMENT and UNCLEARED ITEMS balances change.

☐ Highlight all those items that agree with the bank account statement.

☐ Click on the ADJUSTMENT button to add items that are on the bank statement but not on the computer.

☐ Make sure the BALANCES on the screen now are equal to the bank balance on your statement and save the reconciliation. (Unless, of course, there are items showing on the screen that have not been cleared through the bank in which case they will be included in the UNCLEARED ITEMS box).

Note that any ADJUSTMENTS are written to the NOMINAL LEDGER and will not be reversed even if you abandon the reconciliation before finishing it.

Payment

This is used for payments where the transaction has not been entered in the supplier ledger. The data entry fields are:

Pay to
By clicking on the button to the right of the box, a list of the suppliers you have accounts for will appear. Select the one you want or leave it blank and create a new supplier account.

Date / Cheque No.
Whatever details you need to enter.

N/C / Name
Select a NOMINAL code for the payment and the Name field will be automatically entered.

Description
Enter a description to identify the transaction.

Amount / T/C / VAT Amount
Enter the amount and either accept the default VAT code (T1) or change it and the VAT amount will be calculated for you.

See how the remaining data is entered for you by the program, the Bank Balance at the bottom of the screen is reduced and the amount is entered onto the cheque at the top.

Adding items

You can continue to add items to the payment by moving onto the next data entry row below the one you have filled. Again you will see the other figures automatically increment without you having to do anything else.

It is very useful to be able to see your bank balance at the bottom especially when it becomes a negative figure!

Calculate Net

If you enter the AMOUNT and then click on this button, the VAT is deducted from the payment and entered in the VAT Amount.

This is different from the normal method where the VAT is effectively added to the AMOUNT entered.

Supplier

The data entry fields are:

Pay to

By clicking on the button to the right of the box, a list of the suppliers you have accounts for will appear. Select the one you want, the screen will fill up with the outstanding invoices.

When you select the PAID column, the program defaults to the first in the sequence, if you do not want to pay that one simply move the cursor onto the next (using the cursor keys).

Date / Cheque No.

Whatever details you need to enter.

Tp / Date / Inv. / Description / Amount

These are all entered automatically by the program and display the unpaid or uncleared transactions on that specific supplier's account.

Discount

If you enter the discount in that field then the value in the paid field will alter to take account of this.

The buttons are similar to the PAYMENTS screen except for two, these are:

Pay In Full

If you click on this when in the PAID field the specific item will be cleared and the payment added to the total.

Remittance

If you want to print a remittance advice (before you have saved the data) you can do so by clicking on this button.

Receipt

Again this is for use where the item has not been entered into the customer's ledger.

Deposit No.

Here you can enter the cheque number or other details concerning the receipt.

N/C / Name

Select a nominal code and the name (of it) will be automatically entered.

Description

Text that describes the transaction.

Amount / T/C / VAT

You enter the amount, alter the tax code if necessary and the VAT will be calculated automatically.

Credit card receipts

Nowadays many businesses accept credit cards for sales and you may like to consider the following techniques for dealing with them.

☐ Have separate bank account codes for each credit card company you deal with.

☐ Either post the receipts through the RECEIPTS option or if you want to record the invoice then you will need to enter those details through the CUSTOMER or INVOICING options.

☐ You can transfer the amounts from these special bank accounts to your main account by using the TRANSFER option or by JOURNALISING the amounts.

☐ Any charges made by the credit card company can be adjusted for when you carry out the BANK RECONCILIATION. It is worthwhile using a NOMINAL ACCOUNT CODE for these charges and code 7906 can be set up as being for CREDIT CARD CHARGES (as suggested by SAGE).

Customer

Once you have selected the customer from whom you have received money a list of the amounts outstanding will be displayed.

The data to be entered is similar to previous screens, some of it is entered by the program.

When you select the PAID column, the program defaults to the first in the sequence, if you do not want to pay that one simply move the cursor onto the next (using the cursor keys).

Enter the amount to be paid from the invoice or click on the PAY IN FULL button.

Enter as many items as you want to and then SAVE the data.

Transfer

This enables you to transfer money from one bank account to another.

Statement

You can preview, print or send the bank statement to a file for future use.

Recurring

This lets you deal with recurring entries, the data entry screen is shown below.

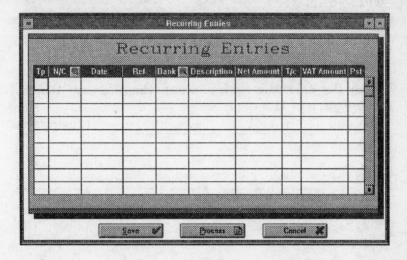

The idea is that you let SAGE deal with entries that occur on a regular basis. The fields are as follows:

Tp
You have a choice of four entries.

| BP / BR | Bank payment or bank receipt |
| JD / JC | Journal debit or journal credit |

N/C / Date / Ref
Enter the relevant data into each of these.

Bank
The bank account you want the entry to be entered into.

Description
A text description.

Net Amount / T/C / VAT Amount
Enter the NET AMOUNT, alter the TAX CODE if necessary and the AMOUNT will be calculated for you.

Pst
A Y entry here shows that the entry has been processed. This is automatically entered by the program.

When the data has been entered, you can save it and PROCESS it.

If you do not process the recurring entries then an error message will appear when you try to run the MONTH END option.

Products

This section deals with recording the stock you hold.
The initial screen looks like this.

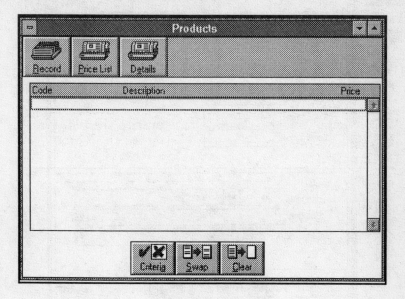

As you can see there only three choices.

Record

In a similar way to the other modules you use this option to record the stock or product items you carry. The screen is shown below.

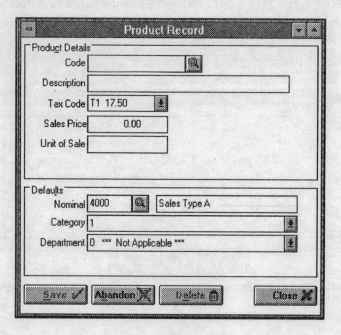

You have to use the RECORD option to start the process of entering stock, it can also be used to make any amendments or to delete unwanted items.

Warning

☐ It is vitally important to think how you want your stock organised and to spend time working out the most logical and usable system before starting to enter the stock.

☐ Pay particular attention to the codes you use. Remember that you may well introduce or buy new stock items as you expand.

Code

This is the code you wish to assign to that particular stock item. It must be unique and can be up to 16 characters long. You can use **F4** or click on the symbol to the right of the field to see the codes already existing.

Description

A description of the product, up to 30 characters can be used.

Tax Code

The VAT code; normally **T1** that represents the normal VAT rate or one of the other VAT codes if the item is not subject to VAT at the standard rate. Clicking on the arrow to the right of the box will bring up a list of the codes you have created.

Sales Price

This is the selling price per unit of the product, that is the current price **net** of VAT.

Unit of Sale

How many of the items are sold together, for example a pair.

Nominal

The nominal code allocated to this product, this is normally one of the Sales codes (the 4000 series).

Category

You can organise your stock into different categories, for example bicycles, tyres, sundries, etc. Remember that these can be set up or altered by using the DEFAULTS menu (along the top of the screen) and then selecting PRODUCT CATEGORIES.

Department
The department that the item will be allocated to.

Price List
This option enables you to display the price list in various ways as you can see from the illustration below.

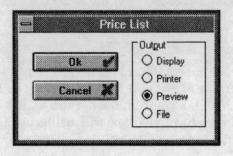

Details
The Product Details option works in exactly the same way as the Price List, enabling you to look at a list of the product details. The screen is very similar to that shown for Price List.

Invoicing

To produce invoices for your customers you use this option, you can also automatically update the Sales (Customers) Ledger. The opening screen is shown below.

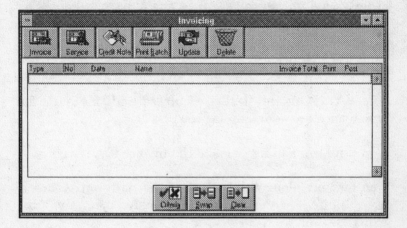

Invoice

Within this you can produce invoices for customers from your stock records.

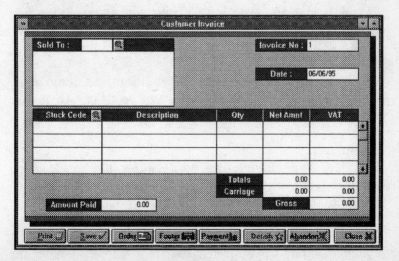

You can enter a NON-STOCK item by using any of the following codes in the STOCK CODE field.

If you enter any of these an additional dialog box will appear into which you can enter details of the non stock item.

S1	Taxable non stock item
S2	Zero rated non stock item
M	Text only

The VAT is automatically calculated and the totals for the invoice are added up for you.

You can keep adding items to the invoice if you wish.

The buttons along the bottom of the data entry screen are different from those previously met and are explained below.

Print
This will print the invoice.

Save
This will save the details and clear the screen ready for the next invoice. After choosing CLOSE the original screen will appear with details of the saved invoices.

You can edit (change) them by highlighting them and then selecting the INVOICE button or delete them by using the DELETE button if you so wish.

Order
This lets you change the address for the goods and invoices from that of the original that you set up when you created the customer record.

Footer

This lets you add certain additional charges to the invoice, any additional carriage and any settlement terms you want to add (as shown below).

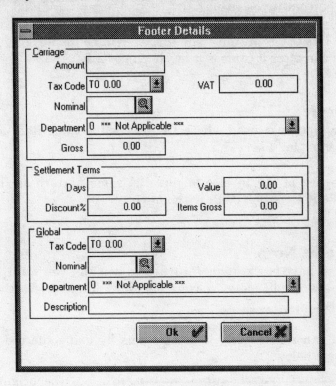

The GLOBAL section enables you to code the whole invoice to a specific TAX or NOMINAL code and DEPARTMENT if you so wish.

Payment

If the customer has made any payments in advance towards this invoice then this can be recorded by selecting the PAYMENT button.

Details

This option enables you to add comments or to amend any of the displayed details.

Abandon / Close

ABANDON lets you clear the screen to enter the details again, CLOSE returns you to the previous screen.

To edit an invoice you have created, simply highlight it within the first INVOICING screen and then click on the INVOICE button. The invoice will be displayed and you can alter it (unless it has been posted).

Service

This option is used where there is not a stock item for example for a service.

The rest of the invoice follows the same pattern as the INVOICE option dealt with above.

Credit Note

If you have stock items returned to you and you want to issue a credit note to your customer then select this option.

You can also enter non-stock items by using the codes shown below.

S1	Taxable non stock item
S2	Zero rated non stock item
M	Text only

The data entry screen is similar to the original stock one and you deal with it in the same way.

You should make sure the codes are the same as the original.

Print Batch

You can select to print one or all of them by selecting the invoices.

Update

It is very important to do this as your ledgers will not be updated otherwise.

This process generates a report that will tell you if the invoice has not been posted and why, it is best to print this report and read it.

Note that you can only update an invoice to the ledger once.

Delete

You can delete any of the displayed invoices or credit notes by highlighting them and then selecting this button. You will be pleased to know that like most of the delete commands this contains a fail-safe where you will be asked to confirm the deletion.

However this is not a good idea once you have updated (posted) the ledgers. Deleting a posted invoice does **not** reverse the posting.

Financials

The actual accounts that you produce are included in this section.

We will look at each of these in sequence starting with the Trial Balance.

Trial (Balance)

This lists the balances on the different nominal ledger accounts you have set up and entered data.

There are two buttons at the bottom of this window allowing you to print the trial balance, or if you select CANCEL you will be returned to the previous menu.

P & L / Balance (Sheet)

Clicking on either of these produces a dialog box that displays the current month. You can alter this to any month you wish.

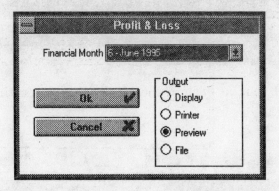

You then have a choice of displaying the resulting set of accounts on the screen, you can print them (or preview them) either on the printer or to a file for future use.

The resulting display shows the selected month and the cumulative figures for the year to date.

Budget

This, again, produces a monthly report of the budget, the actual figures and the variance (difference between the actual and budgeted figures) for both the selected month and the year to date.

Layout

The dialog box that results from selecting this is shown on the next page.

Code Groupings
The groups of codes for the accounts can be altered to suit your organisational needs.

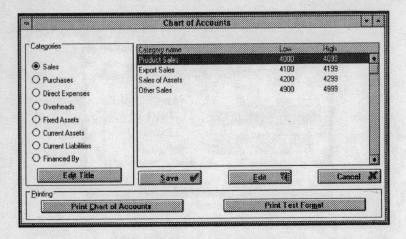

You select a category and the relevant account codes within that category will be displayed on the right of the window. Remember that this may have an affect on your final accounts.

You can EDIT the actual description of each code and the range of numbers applicable to that code by clicking on the EDIT buttons.

Print Chart Of Accounts
This is not as you may think a bar chart of the figures but a list of the account codes used.

Print Test Format
Similar to the chart above only this time you get a list of the ranges rather than each code.

VAT Return

Your VAT return will be calculated automatically for you if you use this option. The choices are:

Calculate

You will need to click on the CALCULATE button to make the program look through the transactions for the period and produce a VAT return for you.

Check the figures against the Sales and Purchase Tax Control Accounts and if there is any discrepancy, you will need to find out why.

Reconcile

This sets a flag (or marker) to the items included within the current VAT return. This means that they will not be included again unless you want them to be by clicking on the INCLUDE RECONCILED TRANSACTIONS button.

You can then look at the detailed breakdown of each figure by clicking in the appropriate box and a screen showing the breakdown will be displayed. A further breakdown can then be displayed by selecting the appropriate button along the bottom of that window.

It is suggested that you **zero** the tax control accounts at the end of each month. This will mean that you are only dealing with one month's figures at a time and will, therefore, find the task of reconciling your figures easier.

To zero the tax codes simply find the balance on the PURCHASE and SALES TAX CONTROL ACCOUNTS and transfer the balances to the VAT LIABILITY ACCOUNT using the NOMINAL JOURNAL option.

You must keep all your reports and work on the VAT return and its reconciliation for inspection by the C&E.

Prior

This is similar to the BUDGET report described earlier, only this time the previous year's figures are included.

Reports

This section of the program enables you to alter or display the default reports or you can create your reports, in whatever layout and with the contents you want.

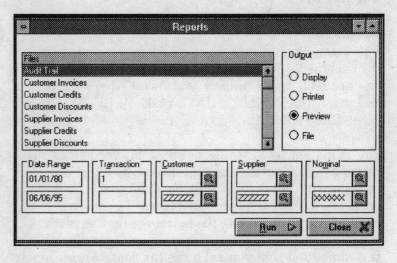

This is, therefore, a very powerful tool for anyone wanting a specific report not catered for already.

There are various boxes just above the buttons and these can be left or they can be altered to the specific data you want to enter (either by typing or clicking on the view symbol to the right of the box and then selecting your choice(s)).

Report files can be saved in a variety of formats, this applies to all reports whether generated from within the Ledgers or the Report module itself.

Below is shown the choice of filetypes (you select the filetype according to the program you want to import it into).

```
Report File (*.RPT)
Write File (*.WRI)
Text File (*.TXT)
CSV File (*.CSV)
```

Computerising Your Accounts

You should never install an accounting system without planning, it is not like a word processing program or a spreadsheet.

There are various ways to do this, and the following suggestions may help you plan.

It is best to install the system at the start of your financial year or at the end of a VAT period.

As a first step (before you begin to use the program live) you should install the names and other details of your suppliers, customers, stock types and other standing information.

One of the more difficult activities is setting up the Coding Structure. If you are unsure about this it is worth money to get a professional to help you. If you create a messy system it will be inefficient to use and costly to alter.

At the end of one accounting year and the beginning of the next extract the balances on all your accounts and then enter them into the new accounting system. Obviously this will take a few days and may need your accountant's help.

Always run parallel systems for a time (this means running both the old manual and the new computerised systems side by side).

This is time consuming and costly but is a necessary security procedure if things go wrong. By checking the manual records against the computer versions you can clear up any misunderstandings and gain confidence at the same time.

Remember not to be too ambitious, it may be best to begin with the Sales Ledger (CUSTOMERS) and when this is working well, then to install the Purchase Ledger (SUPPLIERS). By this time you will be more confident and may like to computerise the NOMINAL Ledger and PRODUCTS.

Setting up SAGE

When you set up your accounting systems onto a computer for the first time there is a specific sequence of activities.

Setting The Financial Year

Not all companies have the same financial year end so the first activity is to set the start of the financial year for your company. Click on the DEFAULTS command along the top of the window and then select FINANCIAL YEAR.

You cannot alter this date once you have entered any data.

Enter Details Of Your Customers And Suppliers

The next step is to enter the details of your existing customers and suppliers.

Print out a list for reference purposes.

Enter The Amounts Due From Customers And The Amounts Due To Suppliers

These are best entered as individual balances for each invoice as they can more easily be allocated when payment is made and will also show up correctly analysed when displaying aged debtors or creditors reports.

You can do this when creating the customer or supplier record by using the SETUP option within that screen.

However SETUP does not provide any VAT analysis nor are the balances analysed to individual nominal accounts so it may be best to use the INVOICE section of the modules.

Enter the date of the invoice (not the system date).

For VAT the normally recommended method is to enter the gross amount and use VAT code **T9** as the VAT should have been dealt with in previous VAT periods.

If you are using VAT CASH ACCOUNTING then you **must** enter them as individual transactions using the INVOICE (CREDIT NOTE) options within the CUSTOMERS or SUPPLIERS modules and entering the appropriate VAT codes. You must **not** use the SETUP options.

Dealing With The Control Accounts

Entering the amount due to suppliers and from customers generates a balance on the SUSPENSE account and this will also appear on the Trial Balance when it is displayed.

These **must** be cleared BEFORE entering the list of ledger balances otherwise they will appear twice.

To display the Trial Balance (from the main menu) select FINANCIALS and then TRIAL and a list of the balances will appear.

WRITE THESE DOWN (there should only be three, the Debtors Control, the Creditors Control and the Suspense Account).

Before doing anything else it is necessary to remove these balances (the record of who owes money to who will be retained).

To do this go back to the main menu and select NOMINAL, then JOURNALS. Enter the data in the opposite way to the way it is shown in the TRIAL BALANCE (remembering to alter the date if necessary).

Thus if it is a DEBIT balance in the TRIAL BALANCE then enter it as a CREDIT balance in the JOURNAL.

It is important to realise that you cannot SAVE a journal UNTIL it balances, in other words the total value of the debit column equals the total of the credit column. The results of the journal will be posted and the trial balance should have no values in it any more.

Close down the open windows and then display or print the TRIAL BALANCE **before** proceeding. Check there is no balance on the SUSPENSE account (A/C code 9998) or on any other account.

| This is a once only operation. |

Set Up The Nominal Ledger
Finally to finish the actual preparation work before you can enter the actual transactions, it is best to set up the NOMINAL codes to reflect your type of work by giving them the names you use in your business and (possibly) delete the ones you will not ever use.

Entering The Opening Trial Balance

When you computerise your accounts you will need to enter the opening Trial Balance (the list of ledger balances that derive from the manual accounts you originally used).

Even if you are starting a new business, there will be opening balances to enter, for example the capital you are investing in the business.

To enter these balances, you select the N/C you want and then click on the SETUP button. This will display a dialog box that asks for the amount.

Please note that the date will be the system date (the date you are entering the data UNLESS you alter it to the date you want). I suggest that to avoid confusion you enter a date the day before the start of your accounting year. This means that the balance will show as the Brought Forward figure not as part of the first month's figure.

Click on TRIAL and check the figures carefully against the originals. There should be **no** SUSPENSE balance and the figures should be identical to those you entered.

If you make a mistake you can create a new journal entry to correct it.

You have successfully set up the ledger system now and are ready to begin to enter transaction data.

Stock

Now enter the stock records using the PRODUCTS module and within that the RECORD button.

The Audit Trail

One of the most important parts of any accounting system is the AUDIT TRAIL. This is a list of **every** transaction that has taken place.

It is a record that cannot be altered and is therefore an excellent check on what has been entered. It is used extensively by professional accountants when auditing a system.

To see the audit trail click on the REPORTS button and select AUDIT TRAIL (which should be the first item on the list).

Look at it carefully and you will see how SAGE has processed the transactions. The symbols used as abbreviations on the audit trail and indeed on the other reports are as follows.

SI	Sales invoice
SC	Sales credit
SA	Sales on account
SD	Sales discount
SR	Sales receipt
PI	Purchase invoice
PC	Purchase credit
PA	Purchase on account
PD	Purchase discount
PP	Purchase payment
BP	Bank payment
BR	Bank receipt
CR	Cash receipt
CP	Cash payment
JD	Journal debit
JC	Journal credit

Other Transaction Types

Other types of transactions are shown below, for example the VAT column uses the following codes.

R	Reconciled
N	Unreconciled

There are also some codes specific to stock items and these are described below.

AI / AO	Adjustment in / out
MI / MO	Movement in / out (transfers only)
GR	Goods returned (credit notes)
GO	Goods out (SOP and INVOICING)
GI	Goods in (POP)

Previewing The Reports

One of the new features of the program is being able to PREVIEW and alter the look of the data before printing it.

Previewing lets you alter the fonts and font sizes of the data in various ways. An explanation of each of the buttons follows.

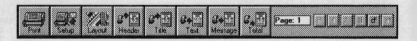

Print
This brings up the standard WINDOWS print dialog box.

Setup
Another standard WINDOWS dialog box that lets you alter various aspects of printing.

Layout
From this you can alter the margin measurements and switch between measuring in inches and centimetres.

Header / Title / Text / Message / Total
You can alter the font (typeface), the size of the type and the format (bold, italic).

Other Buttons
The small buttons to the right are paging (moving from one page to the next or backwards), scrolling (up and down) or zooming in or out (making the image bigger or smaller).

Some of these may be disabled if (for example) the text only fills a single page.

Stationery And Report Layouts

There are several layouts that come with the program. You can use these, you can alter them and save the altered version under a different name or you can create your very own customised layouts.

The following list shows the layouts that come with the program.

LINVOICE.LYT	stock invoices/credit notes
LINVTEXT.LYT	free text invoices
LREMITT.LYT	remittance advices
LSTATMENT.LYT	statements
LLABEL.SLB	customer labels
LLABEL.PLB	supplier labels
LOVERDUE.SAL	overdue letters
LADDRESS.PUR	change of address

You can create your layouts in a similar way to the way you create letters to your customers or suppliers.

Creating New Layouts

Firstly use the **F12** function key to call up the Windows WRITE program and then use the EDIT menu to add the variables, type in any text you want and save the file within the LETTERS directory.

Editing Existing Layouts

As before but this time open the file (FILE and OPEN).
You will find the file in the LETTERS directory.

Hints:

☐ You can add a company logo or any other graphic by PASTING it into your layout.

☐ Save the files with the appropriate extension for the type of file (see the list above).

☐ Backup the original layout files **before** altering them.

The Sage Directory Structure

For information, the program is organised in the following way.

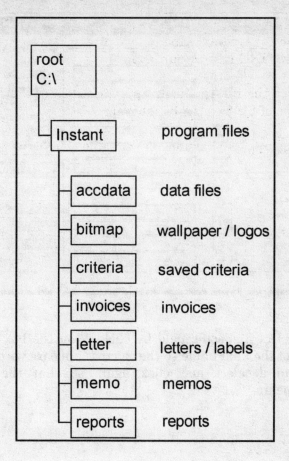

Using Criteria

This lets you choose from all the records the specific ones you want. You do this by choosing certain criteria.

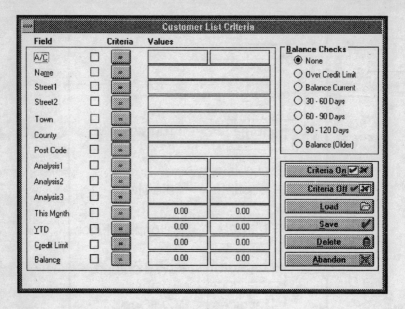

Field

You select a specific field by clicking on the box to the right of the field name so that a cross appears within the box, to deselect just click again so that the cross disappears.

Criteria
The criteria that can be used are:

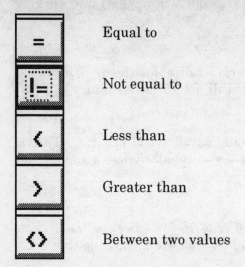

= Equal to

!= Not equal to

< Less than

> Greater than

<> Between two values

You can switch between them by clicking on the symbol and it will change to the next in sequence.

Values
In the value boxes you can use letters or numbers and various other characters, for example

*   A wildcard signifying any character or characters e.g. =TR*

?   This stands for any one character e.g. =?D

$ Checks whether the specified text appears within the field, for example $money or $"fred fawcett" - (if the text includes a space it must be included in inverted commas).

Balance Checks

Similarly with the Balance Checks clicking within the circle turns it on (a large dot will appear) and clicking again turns it off.

Criteria On / Off

This enables the criteria or disables them. If disabled they will still exist but will not affect the data.

Load

You can load an already saved set of criteria. This is obviously time saving if you regularly use a specific set of criteria.

Save

Once you have created criteria you can save them. You will be prompted for a filename when choosing this.

Delete

This enables you to remove any saved sets of criteria.

Abandon

Selecting this clears the criteria you have entered so that you can set new ones.

Entering Dummy Data

This section contains specimen data so that you can practise before using the program. This would be a useful exercise for anyone who is unfamiliar with the program or with accounts.

Please remember that if you decide to enter the dummy data you need to either:

☐ Create a backup **before** entering any data and then restore this or

☐ Re-install the program and data files from the master discs

---

Setting The Financial Year

For the purposes of the exercises within this book, you need to set the year end for your company.

Click on the DEFAULTS command along the top of the window and then select FINANCIAL YEAR. Enter the following date by clicking on the symbol (which is shown to the right of the month).

and then select

```
March
```

Click in the year box and alter it to 1995 as the financial year.

Note: You also need to set the system date to 31/03/95.

Altering The System Date

To do this from within WINDOWS you can use the CONTROL PANEL and then select DATE/TIME. Alter the figures as necessary and then close down the CONTROL PANEL.

Hint:
You can access the CONTROL PANEL by using the function key **F11** from within SAGE.

Entering Details Of Your Customers

Obviously no data can be entered until these have been set up.

Beginning with the Customers, click on the CUSTOMERS icon.

Then click on the RECORD button and a new screen will appear.

You can either use the TAB key to move between the fields or use the mouse to click within each field.

You must click on the SAVE button after completing **each** record. When you have done this the fields will blank ready for you to enter the next record.

If there is no data to be entered just skip over that field.

Enter the data shown on the following page.

A/C	A001	B001
Name	Adams.J	Baskerville.F
Street 1	12 Corn Meadows	3 Daniels Road
Street 2		
Town	Ilfracombe	Ilfracombe
County	Devon	Devon
Post Code	BN56 7T	BN56 9IJ
Contact	Jill Adams	Felix Baskerville
Telephone	0769234541	076943563
Fax		
VAT Reg No		
Last Year		
Credit Limit		
Terms	cash	cash
Due Days		
Nominal	4000	4000
Tax Code	T1	T1

Remember to check the data **before** saving it.

A/C	H001	T001
Name	Happy Holidays	The Hire Shop
Street 1	Broadacres	The Quadrant
Street 2	Chestnut Road	Market Square
Town	Ilfracombe	Ilfracombe
County	Devon	Devon
Post Code	BN56 9IJ	BN56 6F
Contact	Midge Matthews	Kelly Impish
Telephone	076923988	0769119933
Fax	076923983	0769229933
VAT Reg No	897675231	89745012
Last Year	8977.23	2299.65
Credit Limit	5000	2000
Terms	credit	credit
Due Days	30	30
Nominal	4001	4001
Tax Code	T1	T1

When you have finished close down the open windows
(WINDOW and CLOSE ALL).

Entering Details Of Your Suppliers

This is very similar to the CUSTOMERS records. Select the SUPPLIERS icon and then click on RECORD. Enter the data shown below.

A/C	W001	T001
Name	Weelie Wheels	Treck UK
Street 1	45 Cuthbert Road	Oldmile Estate
Street 2		Beckingridge
Town	Saltash	Oldham
County	Devon	Lancs
Post Code	PL8 7YT	MN3 78T
Contact	Harry Hitchens	Polly Ketting
Telephone	0777987698	0364331192
Fax	0777557698	0364341722
VAT Reg No	889966333	19080622
Last Year	9800.23	8765.21
Credit Limit	10000	10000
Terms	credit	credit
Due Days	30	30
Nominal	5001	5000
Tax Code	T1	T1

Note that code T001 is used in both the CUSTOMERS and SUPPLIERS ledgers, this is perfectly acceptable if you wish to do it.

When you have finished close down all the open windows and return to the main menu.

Entering The Amounts Due From Customers

Firstly click on the CUSTOMERS button and then on RECORD. Use the (magnifying) symbol to the right of the A/C field to call up the list of customers you have already created.

To enter the data, call up each relevant customer record in turn and then click on the SETUP button (to the right of the window).

Enter the following data for the customers, **one** at a time, SAVING the data before entering details of the next.

Notice that there are two invoices for customer **T001**.

Customer	Ref	Date	Invoice	Credit
H001	o/bal	31/01/95	345.23	
T001	o/bal	31/12/94	199.99	
T001	o/bal	28/02/95	20.34	

Close down the open windows.

Entering The Amounts Due To Suppliers

Using the same principles, enter the following for the suppliers.

Supplier	Ref	Date	Invoice	Credit
T001	o/bal	28/02/95	4660.23	
W001	o/bal	31/01/95	976.23	

Close down the open windows.

Setting Up The Nominal Ledger

To finish the actual preparation work before you can enter the actual transactions, it is best to set up the NOMINAL codes to reflect your type of work.

From the main menu click on the NOMINAL button.

Changing The Nominal Codes

Click on the RECORD button and then enter the following changes to the original account names.

To do this either type in the N/C (if it is a new code) or use the magnifying button to the right of the N/C box to display a list of the codes and scroll through the list until you obtain the one you want.

Once you have entered or selected the N/C then tab to the NAME box (below the N/C box) and the default (or original) name for that code will appear (if it is a new code then the box will be blank).

Enter the name and then click on the SAVE button and continue to the next code you want to change.

0020	Workshop equipment
4000	Sales - private
4001	Sales - business
4002	Sales - hire of bikes
4003	Sales - sundries
5000	Purchases - bikes
5001	Purchases - sundries

When you have finished close all the open windows and return to the Main Menu.

Dealing With The Control Accounts

Entering the amount due to suppliers and from customers generates a balance on the SUSPENSE account and this will also appear on the Trial Balance when it is displayed.

These **must** be cleared BEFORE entering the list of ledger balances otherwise they will appear twice.

To display the Trial Balance (from the main menu) select FINANCIALS and then TRIAL and a list of the balances will appear.

Before doing anything else it is necessary to remove these balances (the record of who owes money to who will be retained).

Close the open windows.

Removing The Initial Balances

To do this go back to the main menu and select NOMINAL, then JOURNALS. Enter the data shown below (remembering to alter the date to the 28/02/95).

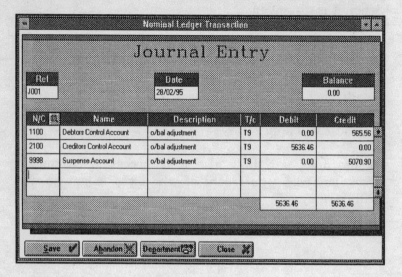

It is important to realise that you cannot SAVE a journal UNTIL it balances, in other words the total value of the debit column equals the total of the credit column.

The results of the journal will be posted and the trial balance should then have no values in it any more.

Save the completed journal entry.

Close down the open windows and then display the TRIAL BALANCE (click on FINANCIALS and then TRIAL) **before** proceeding.

Check there is no balance on the SUSPENSE account (A/C code 9998) or on any other account.

Close down the open windows and return to the main menu.

> If there is a balance on the SUSPENSE account, you have made a mistake and you will need to do another journal to rectify it.

The Opening Trial Balance

Firstly click on the NOMINAL button and then on the RECORD button.

To enter these balances, you select the N/C you want from the list below and then click on the SETUP button. This will display a dialog box that asks for the amount.

Set the date for the 28/02/95

Save the SETUP entry and then save each record and a new blank record will be displayed.

N/C	Name	Debit	Credit
0010	Freehold Property	10000.00	
0020	Workshop equipment	2500.00	
0030	Office equipment	2300.00	
0050	Motor vehicles	4500.00	
1001	Stock	2060.00	
1100	Debtors Control Account	565.56	
1200	Bank Current Account		4591.02
1230	Petty cash	34.89	
2100	Creditors Control Account		5636.46
2202	VAT Liability		78.23
3100	Reserves		11654.74

Close down the open windows and return to the main menu and then select FINANCIALS.

Click on TRIAL and check the figures carefully against the originals. There should be **no** SUSPENSE balance and the figures should be identical to those you entered from the table above.

You have successfully set up the ledger system now and are ready to begin to enter transaction data.

Close down the open windows and return to the main menu.

Products

Recording Your Stock

To begin click on the PRODUCTS button and then on RECORD.

Remember to save each record before proceeding to the next.

Code	PUMA20TR	PUMA16TR
Description	Puma ATB 20"	Puma ATB 16"
Sales Price	349.99	349.99
Unit of Sale	1	1
Nominal	4000	4000

Code	TIGER18TR	TIGER20TR
Description	Tiger ATB 18"	Tiger ATB 20"
Sales Price	549.99	549.99
Unit of Sale	1	1
Nominal	4000	4000

Code	ZONETYRES	BRAKECABLES
Description	Zone 26" tyres	Brake Cables
Sales Price	9.99	.99
Unit of Sale	1	1
Nominal	4003	4003

Close down the open window and then (still within PRODUCTS) select PRICE LIST.

Check that the output is set to PREVIEW and then click on the OK button.

Check the display and then close down all the open windows.

Entering Invoices To Customers

The next activity is to create invoices to send to your customers, select INVOICING from the main menu, followed by INVOICE.

Each customer will require a new invoice form so you should remember to SAVE each as you create it (before moving on to the next).

Sold To	B001	H001
Name	Baskerville.F	Happy Holidays
Date	01/03/95	23/03/95
Stock Code	TIGER18TR	BRAKECABLES
Details	Tiger18TR 18"	5 Brake cables
Net Amount	549.99	4.95
T/c	T1	T1
Footer N/C		4001

Please note that for the second item (BRAKECABLES) you need to select the FOOTER button and alter the **global** NOMINAL code to 4001. This is because it was originally set up as 4000 but this is a business customer not a private one)

The following are SERVICE invoices (that is not stock items) and you should use the SERVICE button instead of the INVOICE one.

Sold To	H001	T001
Name	Happy Holidays	The Hire Shop
Date	12/03/95	31/03/95
Details	hire of 5 bikes	hire of 10 bikes
Net Amount	350.00	700.00
T/c	T1	T1
Footer N/C	4002	4002

When you have entered all of these close down all the open windows and return to the main menu.

Entering Invoices From Suppliers

This time select SUPPLIERS from the main menu and then INVOICE.

Enter the following table of data, saving each before proceeding to the next.

A/C	T001	W001
Name	Treck	Weelie Wheels
Date	04/03/95	06/03/95
Ref	TR3941	WW3999
N/C	5000	5001
Name	Purchases - bikes	Purchases - sundries
Description	2 Tiger18TR	10 Brake Cables
Amount	600.00	5.00
T/c	T1	T1

Again when you have finished entering both sets of data, then close all the open windows and return to the main menu.

Receiving Money From Customers

During March you received the following money from your customers.

To enter this select BANK from the main menu

You will be given a choice of bank accounts, normally you would choose the current account.

Then choose CUSTOMER.

You need to enter the data shown below. After entering the A/C field, the DATE and the REF(erence), click on the relevant PAID field and then on the PAY IN FULL button.

SAVE each and then enter the next and so on and when finished close all the open windows and return to the main menu.

A/C	H001
Name	Happy Holidays
Date	23/03/95
Ref	O/BAL
Paid	345.23

A/C	T001	T001
Name	The Hire Shop	The Hire Shop
Date	05/03/95	15/03/95
Ref	O/BAL	O/BAL
Paid	199.99	20.34

Paying Money To Your Suppliers

Very similar to the receiving of money from customers only this time select SUPPLIER rather than customers **after** selecting BANK.

Enter the following data, again SAVE each before proceeding to the next.

To enter the amount you can click the mouse in the PAID box next to the relevant amount and then click on the PAY IN FULL button. When finished close all the open windows and return to the main menu.

Pay To	T001	W001
Name	Treck UK	Weelie Wheels
Date	31/03/95	31/03/95
Cheque No.	760001	760002
Amount	4660.23	976.23

A Little Practice

New Customers
During March we started dealing with the following new customers.

A/C	C001	T002
Name	Centre Park	Terry Tompkins
Street 1	Everglades	54b Church St.
Street 2	Hill Bottom	
Town	Nr. Barnstaple	Ilfracombe
County	Devon	Devon
Post Code	BT78 7YR	BN21 66R
Contact	Jilly Furnace	Terry Tompkins
Telephone	0444231232	0769814196
Fax	0444231233	
VAT Reg No	777212198	
Credit Limit	5000	
Terms	credit	cash
Due Days	30	
Nominal	4001	4000
Tax Code	T1	T1

Close the open windows after the data.

Sales to Customers

During March we sold the following items to our customers.

Enter these using the INVOICING module (the first item should be entered using the SERVICE button).

Sold To	C001	T002
Name	Centre Park	Tompkins Terry
Date	31/03/95	31/03/95
Details	2 hire bikes	Tiger ATB 18"
Amount	140.00	549.99
T/c	T1	T1
Footer N/C	4002	

Close all the open windows after clicking on the UPDATE button within the INVOICING module.

Purchases from Suppliers

During March the following additional items were bought from our suppliers. Enter these into SUPPLIERS (INVOICE).

Remember to add the new item to the PRODUCTS list.

A/C	T001
Name	Treck UK
Date	05/03/95
Ref	TR5543
N/C (invoice)	5001
Name	Purchases - sundries
Description	Treck Max tyres
Number purchased	10
Amount/Cost	11.99 (each)
Sale Price	15.99 (each)
T/c	T1
Unit of Sale	1
Nominal code	4000

Close all the open windows.

Money Received From Customers

We also received the following cheques from our customers during March.

A/C	T002
Name	Tompkins Terry
Date	31/03/95
Ref	SHOPTT
Amount	646.24

Money Paid To Suppliers

During the month we also paid the following to our suppliers.

A/C	T001	W001
Name	Treck	Weelie Wheels
Date	31/03/95	31/03/95
Cheque No.	760003	760004
Amount	705.00	5.88

Close all the open windows.

Payments From The Bank

As well as payments to suppliers you have to make other payments through the bank.

As these are new accounts click on the SUPPLIERS RECORD button and enter the following details for each supplier.

A/C	BT	SWEB
Name	British Telecom	SWEB
Town	Plymouth	Plymouth
County	Devon	Devon
Postcode	PL23 7TR	PL2 7RT

A/C	CE
Name	Customs & Excise
Town	Plymouth
County	Devon
Postcode	PL9 7YT

Enter the payments below by selecting BANK (choosing the correct bank account) and then PAYMENT.

Make use of the CALCULATE NET button (for the first two items **only**) to work out the net amount as you have only been given the gross amount.

Save each before going on to the next.

Pay To	BT	SWEB	CE
Date	31/03/95	31/03/95	31/03/95
Cheque No.	760005	760006	760007
N/C	7502	7200	2202
Name	Telephone	Electricity	VAT liability
Description	March – September	March – June	o/s VAT
Amount	424.23	489.11	78.23
Tax Code	T1	T1	**T9**

Close all the open windows.

Recurring Entries (Bank)

Most businesses have recurring entries, these are amounts that have to be paid regularly.

To obtain this, firstly select the BANK and then RECURRING.

Enter the following data (BP stands for bank payment).

Tp	BP	BP
N/C	7102	7103
Date	01/03/95	01/03/95
Ref	wr1995	gr1995
Bank	1200	1200
Description	water rates	general rates
Net Amount	20.00	75.00
T/c	T9	T9

Enter both of these (on the same screen) and then click on the PROCESS button.

Note: Recurring entries can only be processed for the **current** month.

You should be able to see the transaction if you look at the bank account by closing down the open windows and then selecting NOMINAL.

Click on the code for the BANK CURRENT ACCOUNT (1200) and then click on the ACTIVITY button followed by the HISTORY button.

Scroll down the list and you should see that the recurring transactions for the month have been processed (at the bottom).

Close down all the open windows.

The monthly accounts

So far you have set up the opening details of the business, you have entered invoices received and sent and have recorded money you have paid and received. Now it's time to start looking at the various reports and accounting information you can get from the system.

From the main menu choose FINANCIALS and then TRIAL. This will list all the NOMINAL accounts with a balance on them.

Adjusting for VAT

Another end of month adjustment that it is sensible to make is to clear the balances on the SALES and PURCHASE TAX CONTROL ACCOUNTS by transferring the balances to the VAT LIABILITY ACCOUNT.

This will let you start the next month with nothing on the SALES and PURCHASE TAX CONTROL ACCOUNTS and you will be able to agree your VAT return more easily month by month. You will also be clear about how much you owe to the Customs and Excise.

Look at the balances for the SALES and PURCHASE TAX CONTROL accounts and write the balances down (by looking at the Trial Balance).

The journal entries for this month are as follows.

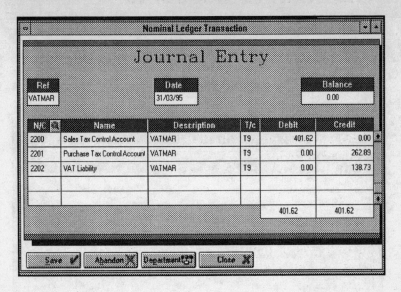

Again SAVE the journal and then close all the open windows.

The Trial Balance

After entering these, you should print out or display the TRIAL BALANCE again (FINANCIALS and then TRIAL).

This time the figures have changed slightly and look like this.

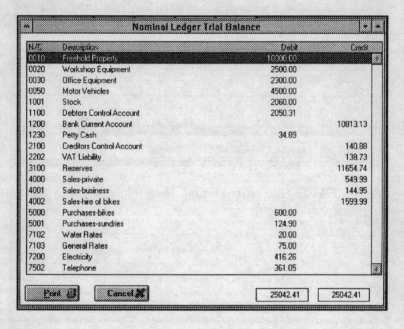

To look at the profit (or loss) select P&L after selecting FINANCIALS.

To see the Balance Sheet select BALANCE. Display or print it out.

Each of these financial statements can be displayed on the screen or printed. Generally printing it out makes it easier to read.

The VAT Return

To finish our initial look at the accounts, select VAT (from FINANCIALS).

Click on the CALCULATE button and on the OK button. Then click on the RECONCILE button and answer YES to the question. This marks or flags the items that have been entered onto the VAT return so that they will not be used again.

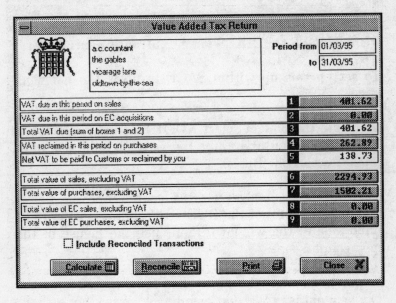

You will see the likeness of an official VAT form appears on the screen already completed. A real bonus as you can now print it.

Close down the open windows.

Budgeting

As well as producing the accounts (trial balance, profit and loss account and the balance sheet), your accounting records can be used to provide useful information to aid your business decisions.

One of these features is the use of budgets to produce variance analysis. A variance is the difference between what you spent and the budget you set for that item.

To practise you are going to set up a budget for PURCHASES OF BIKES for the current financial year.

To set up this up within SAGE involves the following steps.

To create the budget select NOMINAL and click on the RECORD button and enter the account code you want (5000 Purchases - Bikes).

Then enter the budget for the year (enter the figure 8000) in the total of the BUDGET column (on the right hand side of the window), then click the mouse in the next column.

You will see that the figure has been spread over the twelve months of the year equally.

Now click on the GRAPHS button along the bottom of the window and you will see a graph of the figures.

Click on the PREV YEAR box along the bottom left of the window so that there is no X in the box (as you do not have any previous year's figures).

You should now have a column (or bar chart) showing the budgeted and actual figures for the first month of the year and the budget for the remainder of the year.

Close down the chart and then save the revised record with the budgeted figures and then close this window.

Close all the open windows.

Reports

You can generate reports from most of the individual modules within SAGE. They can be printed, displayed on the screen, previewed or saved to file.

To look at this feature of the program, you are going to generate some reports.

Nominal Reports

Click on the NOMINAL button and you will see a list of all the nominal codes. Highlight the code 1200 (BANK CURRENT ACCOUNT) and then click on the REPORT button.

Displaying The Report

Make sure that the DISPLAY is marked with a filled circle.

Then click on the RUN button and the report will be displayed on the screen.

After looking at this, close it down and return to the dialog box.

Previewing The Report

A very useful feature of the report is being able to preview it and alter the appearance. This will affect the look of the report, whether it is displayed on the screen or printed.

To do this alter the OUTPUT to PREVIEW and then RUN the report.

Note the two zoom buttons in the top right of the window.

These are used to make the report larger or smaller on the screen (be careful not to make it too large to see all the data).

Alter the fonts for the HEADER, TITLE, TEXT and TOTAL to a larger size by clicking on the appropriate button and use bold and italic as you wish by clicking on the relevant buttons and altering the font sizes as necessary.

Be careful not to use too large a font so that the figures are not all shown properly.

When satisfied close the windows.

Customised Reports

Within each report dialog box there is an option called
NEW, this lets you create your reports.

Let's look at this within the CUSTOMERS ledger.

Click on the CUSTOMERS button and select REPORT.
Now click on the NEW button.

To create your report simply click on the fields that you
require and then SAVE the new setup with its name
(call it SUPP1), it will be immediately added to the list
of reports.

See how you can include various analysis fields within
the report.

You will see your new report listed as well as the fixed
reports.

PREVIEW your report, alter the fonts as you wish and
when satisfied print it. Close down all the open
windows.

You have now finished entering the dummy data and
you may like to continue to practise or to begin entering
your data.

Index

—D—

Debtors, 6, 7, 8, 13, 54, 58, 65, 66, 100, 101, 122
Default, 32, 34, 39, 54, 56, 75, 96, 118
Department, 36, 53, 57, 69, 86, 89
Dialog Boxes, 15, 23, 24, 25, 88, 93, 103, 106
Directory Structure, 109
Discount, 54, 77, 104

—E—

Errors, 41

—F—

Financial Year, 18, 33, 44, 53, 98, 100, 113, 138
Free Text, 107
Function Keys, 26

—G—

Graphs, 2, 68, 138

—H—

Help, 2, 3, 4, 12, 26, 27, 28, 30, 40, 46, 47, 48, 98

—I—

Icons, 18, 20, 62
Installing, 16, 17
Instant Help, 27, 30
Invoicing, 3, 54, 55, 79, 87, 90, 105, 124, 129

—J—

Journal, 67, 69, 81, 95, 102, 103, 104, 120, 121, 135

—L—

Legal Requirements, 13
Letters, 2, 52, 61, 107, 108, 111
Liabilities, 6, 7, 13, 65, 94

—M—

Month End, 43, 53, 82
Monthly Accounts, 134

—N—

Net Assets, 6, 7
Nominal Codes, 25, 75, 78, 85, 89, 118, 140
Nominal Ledger, 9, 74, 92, 102, 118

—O—

Oops, 41

—P—

Parallel Systems, 28, 98
Password, 21, 31
Petty Cash, 66
Preferences, 31
Preview, 60, 61, 80, 93, 106, 123, 140, 142
Print Batch, 91
Printer Setup, 29
Printing, 136, 137, 142
Products, 3, 83, 103, 123, 130
Profit & Loss, 4, 5, 6, 10, 64, 138
Purchase Ledger, 9, 99

—R—

Receipts, 73, 79
Reconcile, 3, 12, 72, 74, 95, 137
Recurring Entries, 81, 82, 133
Restore, 38, 39, 40, 113

—S—

Sales Ledger, 8, 28, 99
Scroll Bars, 15
Security, 38, 98
Statement, 12, 60, 62, 73, 74, 80
Stationery, 20, 52, 64, 66, 107
Suspense Account, 54, 66, 101, 102, 103, 119, 120, 121, 122
System Date, 56, 68, 101, 103, 114

—T—

Tax Codes, 35, 95
Trial Balance, 9, 92, 101, 119, 120, 122, 134, 136, 138
Turnover, 11, 54
Tutorial, 20

—V—

VAT Cash Accounting, 32, 33, 101
VAT Return, 134, 137

—W—

Windows Conventions, 14

—Y—

Year End, 44, 53, 100, 113